# Warm Salads Are A Good Choice!

## They Will Also Warm Up Your Heart!

BY: Ivy Hope

Copyright © 2020 by Ivy Hope

**IVY HOPE**
COOKBOOK

# Copyright/License Page

Please don't reproduce this book. It means you are not allowed to make any type of copy (print or electronic), sell, publish, disseminate or distribute. Only people who have written permission from the author are allowed to do so.

This book is written by the author taking all precautions that the content is true and helpful. However, the reader needs to be careful about his/her action. If anything happens due to the reader's actions the author won't be taken as responsible.

# Table of Contents

Introduction .................................................................................................................. 5

    Warm spinach, bacon and hardboiled eggs salad ............................................. 7

    Warm green beans and mushrooms side salad ............................................... 10

    Warm prosciutto and herbs salad .................................................................... 12

    Warm ham, peas and cheese salad ................................................................. 14

    Tuna on a warm bed of salad .......................................................................... 16

    Warm diced sweet potatoes, dried cranberries and more ............................... 18

    Warm sautéed red skin potatoes ..................................................................... 20

    Asparagus and shrimp warm salad ................................................................. 22

    Super powerful white and red beans salad ..................................................... 25

    Warm and spicy buffalo chicken .................................................................... 27

    The simplest zucchini warm salad .................................................................. 30

    Comforting warm fruits salad ......................................................................... 32

    Kale and sesame warmed up salad ................................................................. 34

    Leftover turkey warm salad ............................................................................ 36

    Garlic, broccoli and lentils warm salad .......................................................... 38

Corn warm salad for everyone ............................................................................... 40

Sausages and much more warm salad ..................................................................... 42

Warm unexpected radish salad ................................................................................ 44

Green and white, parsley and rice warm salad ........................................................ 46

Salmond and citrus warm salad ............................................................................... 48

Warm pasta salad served in an avocado .................................................................. 50

Exceptional Greek warm salad ................................................................................ 52

Beautiful bed of greens with fruits and warm crispy cheese .................................. 54

Warm fried eggs salad .............................................................................................. 56

Goat cheese will warm up your heart ...................................................................... 58

Conclusion ..................................................................................................................... 60

About the Author ........................................................................................................... 62

Author's Afterthoughts .................................................................................................. 63

# Introduction

    Let us explore together a few staples, must-haves in your kitchen and your refrigerator when it's about making some warm salads. You want to be ready at all times, even on a Monday night after a long day at work.

Of course, we do not expect you or anyone else to have at all times fresh fruits and vegetables. We understand that they do perish and you need to limit your purchases in the produce department. However, I personally try to keep at least one bag of prewashed mixed greens. This way, if I do not use it to prepare a salad per say, I can use part of it to dress up sandwiches or tacos. In addition, the basic veggies such as garlic, onions should have a place in your heart and your refrigerator at all times.

In your pantry, however, you should keep more rigid inventory, so when you are feeling like making a yummy warm salad, you can easily make one quick trip to the local produce market and be done.

You should keep some canned tuna or even canned chicken or both. You can also keep canned salmon, but I honestly very rarely use it, I will prefer to bake some fresh salmon and flake it after to add to a salad. In the pantry, you should also always have some nuts (almonds, walnuts, pistachios, pine nuts or any of your favorite). You should also keep a few types of dried fruits, such as dried cranberries, raisons, dates, figs or other.

Additionally, you can add to your stock some fried dried onions, sundried tomatoes, banana peppers, olives and other garnish you would typically top of your salad with.

Finally, in order to dress up your salad, you need some tasty vinaigrettes, and I suggest you keep a few store-bought ones ready to use: ranch, blue cheese, Italian, French or any of your other favorites.

Are you ready to discover some amazing recipes for warm salads and explore so many possibilities for every day of the year! It is time to start!

.

# Warm spinach, bacon and hardboiled eggs salad

You can choose to sauté the spinach and serve some bacon and eggs on top. You can also prepare the bacon and hard-boiled eggs and place them on a fresh, crisp and cold bed of baby spinach leaves. Either way, you get will the wonderful benefits from the spinach and you can top of it off with the bacon greases warm dressing that suggested below.

**Serving Size:** 4

**Cooking Time:** 40 Minutes

**Ingredients:**

- 8 slices of bacon
- 4-5 cups baby spinach leaves
- 4 hardboiled eggs
- 2 minced green onions
- ½ cup shredded Parmesan cheese

**Dressing:**

- 2 Tbsp. Bacon grease
- 2 tbsp. olive oil
- 1 tbsp. minced garlic
- 2 honey mustard
- 4 Tbsp. while balsamic
- Salt, black pepper

**Instructions:**

1. Start by boiling water and prepare the hardboiled eggs as you normally would.

2. Meanwhile, you should cook the sliced bacon in a skillet on the stovetop.

3. Make sure you rinse under cold water the hardboiled eggs when done and peel them without leaving any shell on. Let the eggs cool off and slice.

4. Next, remove the bacon from the skillet and keep the bacon grease in a glass bowl.

5. In the bowl, add all the ingredients listed for the vinaigrette. Set aside.

6. Divide the baby spinach leaves into 4 portions, on 4 places.

7. Add the equivalent of 1 sliced hardboiled egg on top of each one, a few slices of bacon, and sprinkle some Parmesan cheese and green onions.

8. Finally, warm up for a minute in the microwave the bacon grease dressing and drizzle a generous portion top of each salad.

9. Enjoy on a Saturday night with a glass of wine!

# Warm green beans and mushrooms side salad

This is the best salad to make when you can get your hands on fresh green beans. Trim them well and steam them slightly. Use an oily vinaigrette and some additional ingredients such as sautéed mushrooms and garlic.

**Serving Size:** 4

**Cooking Time:** 45 Minutes

**Ingredients:**

- 2 cups fresh green beans
- 2 cups fresh yellow beans
- 1 diced red bell pepper
- 1 Tbsp. minced garlic
- 1/2 cup fried dried onions
- 2 Tbsp. sesame seeds
- ¼-cup sesame oil
- Salt, black pepper
- 1 Tbsp. balsamic vinegar
- 2 Tbsp. teriyaki sauce

**Instructions:**

1. Bring water to boil in a large saucepan, add a little salt and oil.

2. Trim the green and yellow beans after washing them carefully.

3. Place them to boil and steam cook for 10 minutes.

4. You want the beans to be crunchy and vibrant. Drain well.

5. In a skillet heat oil and cook the sesame seeds, diced peppers for 3-4 minutes with the garlic.

6. Combine the beans with the other veggies in a large bowl.

7. In a small mixing bowl, combine the oil, vinegar, teriyaki sauce and spices.

8. Finally, add the sauce to the green beans, mix well, and serve right away while it is warm.

# Warm prosciutto and herbs salad

This pasta salad recipe is just very yummy and comforting. Prosciutto gives such a great salty and rich taste to this salad. In addition, it is important to use fresh herbs for this recipe, so get your scissors and walk to your garden or drive to the produce section of your local grocery store. Finally, make sure you do have plenty of black cracked pepper to add.

**Serving Size:** 4

**Cooking Time:** 50-55 Minutes

**Ingredients:**

- 1 box of uncooked penne pasta
- 1 cups diced prosciutto ham
- 1 tbsp. minced fresh parsley
- 1 Tbsp. minced fresh thyme
- 1 cups shredded Swiss cheese
- ½-cup vegetable broth
- 1 1/2-cup heavy cream
- Salt, black pepper
- 1 tsp. smoked paprika
- 1 Tbsp. unsalted butter

**Instructions:**

1. In a large pot, heat water, oil and salt.

2. Add the uncooked pasta and cook as indicated on the box or as you normally do.

3. Meanwhile, let us make the creamy sauce you will use for this pastas salad.

4. In a medium saucepan, heat some butter and cook the garlic and the fresh herbs together.

5. Add the broth and the cream, cheese and stir until the ingredients blend nicely. Let the sauce simmer for 10 minutes.

6. By then, the pasta must be cooked, drain well.

7. Combine the pasta, sauce, and prosciutto and serve right away.

# Warm ham, peas and cheese salad

This salad is great if you are trying to avoid pasta, bread, rice, or alike starchy foods. I think it's perfect when you have leftover cooked ham and are tired to eat sandwiches or perhaps you just have deli ham meat you need to use up before you switch to turkey. Either size matters. We will dice everything small.

**Serving Size:** 2

**Cooking Time:** 30 Minutes

**Ingredients:**

- 1 1/1 cup diced cooked smoked ham
- ¼-cup sweet peas
- ½ cup diced sharp cheddar cheese
- 1 Tbsp. diced sweet onion
- 2 tbsp. Mayonnaise
- Pinch of salt
- Pinch of black
- Pinch dried mustard

**Instructions:**

1. In s small mixing bowl, combine the mayonnaise and all spices.

2. In a medium mixing bowl, combine the ham, cheese and peas.

3. Add the mayonnaise mixture and then warm up the salad before serving it.

4. You can use the microwave for about a minute or so before serving.

# Tuna on a warm bed of salad

The tuna on your salad will not be what is served warm. The bed of salad is actually what will be slightly warm before you place an excellent tuna salad on top with toppings. Enjoy every bite of it!

**Serving Size:** 3-4

**Cooking Time:** 20-25 Minutes

**Ingredients:**

- 3 medium canned tuna, well drained
- 2 tbsp. Olive oil
- 2 Tbsp. diced black olives
- Salt, black pepper
- 2 tbsp. diced dilled pickles
- 1/4 cup chopped dried sundried tomatoes
- ¼ cup shredded Mozzarella
- 4 cups mixed greens

**Instructions:**

1. Drain the tuna really well and place in a small saucepan. Add the oil, olives, pickles, spices. Keep warm on low temperatures.

2. Meanwhile, in a large bowl, combine the greens, sundried tomatoes and shredded cheese.

3. When you are ready to serve, divide the greens into 4 portions, 4 different plates.

4. Add the warm tuna mixture, after dividing into 4 equal portions.

5. You can also decorate with some fresh parsley if you have some handy.

# Warm diced sweet potatoes, dried cranberries and more

This salad is a perfect fall salad. It includes perfectly sweet potatoes, just sweet enough to make you almost want to eat this salad for dessert. In addition, we will add some nuts, dried fruits and blue cheese. You could eat this salad cold, but I truly recommend it warm, it is much tastier!

**Serving Size:** 4

**Cooking Time:** 60 Minutes

**Ingredients:**

- 4 large peeled sweet potatoes
- 1 cup crumbled blue cheese
- ¼ cup dried cranberries
- ¼ cup roasted pine nuts
- 1 Tbsp. minced fresh parsley
- 3 Tbsp. coconut oil
- Salt, black pepper
- Pinch ground cinnamon

**Instructions:**

1. Peel the potatoes and cook steam cook them a few at a time in the microwave.

2. Do not overcook them. You want them to be firm still and dice them. Place the diced potatoes in a large bowl.

3. In a small mixing bowl, heat the coconut oil and add the spices in it and stir.

4. Add the oil, parsley, nuts and cranberries. Combine.

5. Finally, add the crumbled cheese and use a wooden spoon to stir all ingredients together.

6. Taste and adjust the spices as needed, before serving the warm potatoes salad.

# Warm sautéed red skin potatoes

I think this salad or side dish, as you wish to call it! I do believe you should keep the skin on the potatoes. There are a few reasons why I believe you should: you keep the vitamins and fibers intact, and you keep the red color to toss around in your salad. In addition, we will add some green colors by adding fresh herbs and spices.

**Serving Size:** 4

**Cooking Time:** 45 Minutes

**Ingredients:**

- 4-5 medium red skin potatoes
- 2 tbsp. olive oil
- 2 tbsp. minced fresh sage
- 1 Tbsp. minced garlic
- Salt, black pepper
- 1 tsp. red pepper flakes
- 1 cup chopped pepperoni.
- ½-cup sour cream

**Instructions:**

1. As we mentioned before, you should leave the skin on the red skin potatoes.

2. Wash them throughout and slice them as thin as possible.

3. You will need a large iron skillet for this recipe.

4. Heat up some olive oil and sautéed the garlic, the sage and spices for about 15-18 minutes on medium heat.

5. Add the pepperoni and continue cooking another 5 minutes.

6. Divide the warms potatoes salad into 4 equal portions and serve with sour cream.

# Asparagus and shrimp warm salad

These asparagus is so great. We will bake them with a little olive oil, salt, pepper, and garlic. We will also cook the shrimp that we will add to the green veggies. In addition, some red onions will come into play, adding flavor and additional colorful vibes.

**Serving Size:** 4

**Cooking Time:** 45 Minutes

**Ingredients:**

- 1 pound fresh asparagus
- 1-pound medium peeled, deveined shrimp
- 1 peeled and grated carrot
- 2 cups fresh button mushrooms
- 1 tbsp., garlic minced garlic
- 1/4 cup diced yellow onions
- Lemon wedges
- 1 tbsp. lemon juice
- Olive oil
- Salt, black pepper
- 1 Tbsp. capers

**Instructions:**

1. Preheat the oven to 400 degrees F.

2. Brush olive oil on a baking sheet. Place the asparagus on the sheet and season with salt and pepper.

3. In a large pan, heat the olive oil, sautéed garlic, onions, grated carrots, and mushrooms for 10-12 minutes on medium heat.

4. Finally, add the shrimp and the lemon juice.

5. Continue cooking until the shrimp are done and pink.

6. The asparagus should be baked for no more than 12 minutes or so. When done, cut it in pieces of about 1 inch.

7. Place the warm asparagus in a large mixing bowl.

8. Finally, add the mixed cooked veggies, shrimp, and capers.

9. Adjust the seasonings and add lemon wedges to decorate.

# Super powerful white and red beans salad

You know by now how great beans are for your health. You can find them in different colors and for the purpose of this recipe, we will use the white ones. After second thoughts, we will also add red kidney beans. We will bring all ingredients together with a delicious oil-based sauce.

**Serving Size:** 4

**Cooking Time:** 35-40 Minutes

**Ingredients:**

- 1 can white kidney beans
- 1 can red kidney beans
- 1 small can crushed tomatoes
- 1 small diced yellow bell pepper
- 1 Tbsp. minced garlic
- 2 minced green onion
- Pinch ground cumin
- 1 Tbsp. minced fresh basil
- Salt, black pepper
- 1 tbsp. Lime juice
- Olive oil

**Instructions:**

1. Line up all the ingredients you will need on the kitchen counter.

2. In a large skillet, heat some olive oil on medium heat and start cooking the onions, yellow bell peppers, basil and garlic. Cook for about 10 minutes.

3. Rinse and drain well the white and red beans. Add to the cooked veggies, lime juice, spices and crushed tomatoes.

4. Keep this salad warm until ready to serve.

5. I often serve this salad with some shredded sharp cheddar on top, making it almost like a chili version.

# Warm and spicy buffalo chicken

Feel free to fry, bake, or grill the chicken. About the sauce, we suggest a homemade buffalo sauce. Also, make sure you add some avocado and don't forget to choose your favorite salad dressing to top it off with grace.

**Serving Size:** 4

**Cooking Time:** 40 Minutes

**Ingredients:**

- 1 medium ripped avocado
- 8 chicken uncooked tenders
- ½ cup salty pumpkin seeds
- ¼ cup diced red onions
- ½ seedless sliced cucumbers
- 4-5 cups mixed greens
- Tortilla chips when serving

**Buffalo sauce**

- ½ cup hot sauce (your favorite brand)
- 3 Tbsp. unsalted butter
- 1 Tbsp. white vinegar
- ½ tsp. garlic powder
- Pinch salt and cayenne pepper

**Instructions:**

1. Let us start by making the sauce. In a mixing bowl, combine all the ingredients for the buffalo sauce and set aside for now.

2. Get the chicken out and cut into pieces, so it is easier to cook.

3. Dip each chicken tender into the buffalo sauce. Heat some olive oil and start cooking the chicken until completely done, usually about 12-15 minutes.

4. Meanwhile, combine the mixed greens, red onions, and pumpkin seeds in a large bowl.

5. Divide the salad into 4 plates and add the cooked chicken on top.

6. Finally, add some diced avocado pieces on top and choose your favorite dressing! Also, serve the salad with tortilla chips.

# The simplest zucchini warm salad

You hear this so many times before, I know, the simpler, the better. In this recipe case, it is 100% true. We prepare and present this warm salad in a very humble way but with a very proud head up high way. Spices and lemon juice will be some of the highlights.

**Serving Size:** 4

**Cooking Time:** 30 Minutes

**Ingredients:**

- 2 medium fresh sliced zucchinis
- 1 tbsp. minced garlic
- 2 Tbsp. lemon juice
- 1 tbsp. lemon zest
- 2 diced fresh jalapenos
- Salt, black pepper
- ¼ cup dried fried onions
- Olive oil

**Instructions:**

1. In a large skillet, heat the olive oil and cook the garlic for 3 minutes before adding the jalapenos and the sliced zucchinis.

2. Add the spices on the veggies and the lemon juice and lemon zest.

3. Continue cooking for another 10 minutes or so.

4. Serve the warm zucchinis salad, add some fried onions toppings.

# Comforting warm fruits salad

This may be a first for you. I hcreated this salad many years ago. I used to serve warm oatmeal or warm grits or even quinoa with fruits on top. Most of the time, the fruits were cool or even cold in some cases. My kid's biggest complaints were that the contrast in temperatures was unpleasant and they did not like it. Therefore, I decided to propose a warm combination of fruits, with or without cereals. It is a warm fruit salad.

**Serving Size:** 4

**Cooking Time:** 45 Minutes

**Ingredients:**

- 1 cup fresh blueberries
- 1-cup fresh sliced strawberries
- 1-cup fresh raspberries
- ¼ cup orange juice
- 1 large can of peaches in juice
- 2 cups uncooked quinoa
- 4 cups orange juice
- 1 tbsp. unsalted butter
- 1 tsp. ground cinnamon

**Instructions:**

1. Boil the orange juice, butter and cinnamon together.

2. Add the uncooked quinoa and cook as you normally would quinoa. This means that after the quinoa is added, the temperature needs to be turned to low and let it cook for 20-25 minutes or until done.

3. Meanwhile, wash and drain all fresh fruits.

4. In a medium saucepan, add all the peaches, juice, and all berries. Keep the fruits warm until you are ready to serve it.

5. Place some quinoa on bottom of the bowl, add the warm fruits mixture, and perhaps some Greek yogurt on top or even whipped cream if you are daring.

# Kale and sesame warmed up salad

Kale is so good for you. Dark green vegetables are so great for you, eat them as much as you can. This warm salad is easy to make and the same taste in it will make you forget any other unpleasant taste you may have experienced before.

**Serving Size:** 4

**Cooking Time:** 30 Minutes

**Ingredients:**

- 4-6 cups chopped kale
- 1 Tbsp. garlic
- 1 tsp. onion powder
- 1/2 cup toasted sliced almonds
- 2 tbsp. unsalted butter
- Salt, black pepper

**Instructions:**

1. Preheat the oven to 400 degrees F. Lay the sliced almonds on the baking sheet and roast them until they are simply golden, maybe 10-15 minutes.

2. In a large skillet, heat the butter and cook the garlic for 5 minutes.

3. Add the chopped kale and continue cooking for another 10 minutes. Add the rest of the butter and the spices. Stir and cook another 5 minutes on medium heat.

4. When serving, add a handful of roasted almonds on top and enjoy warm.

# Leftover turkey warm salad

Let us use your leftovers wisely. Using turkey to make several meals after you have cooked a large turkey and are left with several containers full of meat should be a privilege. You can make some turkey pot pie, soup, sandwiches. Today, we ware, however, making this wonderful turkey warm salad, follow our lead.

**Serving Size:** 2

**Cooking Time:** 30 Minutes

**Ingredients:**

- 2 cups cooked turkey meat
- 1 tbsp. coconut oil
- 2 tbsp. golden raisins
- 2 fresh sliced Bartlett pears
- ½ tsp. garlic powder
- ½ smoked paprika

**Instructions:**

1. In the saucepan, warm up the coconut oil at low temperatures. Add the spices.

2. Add the cooked turkey, golden raisins.

3. Combine all the ingredients well and then divide the mixture into two bowls.

4. Slice the pears and place on top or side of the salad.

5. Eat with warm turkey salad with crackers or pita chips.

# Garlic, broccoli and lentils warm salad

Instead of laying your lentils on a bed of green leaves, you can use green broccoli florets. The broccoli offers so many vitamins, minerals, and lentils offer so many proteins. This salad can be served as a meal for sure.

**Serving Size:** 4

**Cooking Time:** 40 Minutes

**Ingredients:**

- 1 fresh broccoli head, cut into florets
- 2 medium cans of lentils, well rinsed and drained
- ¼ cup chopped sweet onions
- 1 tbsp. minced garlic
- 1 cup crumbled Feta cheese
- Salt, black pepper
- 1 tsp. red pepper flakes
- 1 Tbps. unsalted butter

**Instructions:**

1. Boil water in a medium saucepan and steam cook the broccoli for about 12 minutes or until the broccoli is cooked but still crunchy.

2. Meanwhile, in a pan, heat the butter and cook the onions and garlic for about 7-8 minutes. Add the lentils to the veggies, as well as all the spices.

3. When the broccoli is done, place right away in a serving bowl, while it is steaming hot.

4. Add the lentils mixture and combine all together.

5. Divide the salad into 4 portions.

6. Add the crumbled Feta cheese into the 4 bowls as well.

7. Enjoy!

# Corn warm salad for everyone

There is no bad way to warm up corn. You can just place it in a small pot and warm it up, serve as it, maybe with a little butter. You can also transform it into this delicious, vibrant warm salad: add some cilantro, some red onions, maybe some avocados, tomatoes or even some cooked ground beef.

**Serving Size:** 3-4

**Cooking Time:** 30 Minutes

**Ingredients:**

- 3 cups kernel corn
- 1 large diced ripe peeled avocado
- 3 tbsp. Diced red onions
- 1 cup diced fresh tomatoes
- 2 tbsp. Sliced black olives
- 1 Tbsp. minced fresh cilantro
- 1 tbsp. lime juice
- 1 Tbsp. olive oil
- 1 Tbsp. red pepper flakes
- 1 cup cubed sharp Cheddar
- Pinch salt

**Instructions:**

1. In a small mixing bowl, combine the olive oil, lime juice, red pepper flakes, cilantro. Set aside.

2. In a large skillet, place the corn. Add the onions, olives and start warming it up on low temperature.

3. Add the oil mixture and then the fresh tomatoes as well.

4. Finally, prepare the avocado by dicing it and sprinkle a little lime juice on top.

5. Serve into 4 different bowls and add a few pieces minced of cilantro if you like to decorate.

# Sausages and much more warm salad

This recipe will wake your taste buds if nothing else does. Smoked sausages and dill flavors will marry so well. However, we will add so many more ingredients that will marry well and create an amazing warm salad you can serve to your guests when they show up unexpectedly.

**Serving Size:** 4

**Cooking Time:** 50 Minutes

**Ingredients:**

- ½ box uncooked shell pasta
- 3 cups vegetable broth
- 2 large smoked turkey sausage, or your very favorite kind
- 1 Tbsp. olive oil
- ½ tsp. garlic powder
- ½-onion powder
- ½ tsp. smoked paprika
- 1 medium diced green bell pepper
- 2 tbsp. Minced fresh dill
- 3 tbsp. Italian dressing, your favorite brand

**Instructions:**

1. Boil the broth in a medium saucepan and then cook the pasta s you normally wood.

2. Slice the smoked sausage and set aside. I like to slice them as thin as possible, so they cook quicker.

3. Meanwhile, in a skillet, heat a little olive oil and cook the sliced sausage for about 15 minutes or until done, stirring often.

4. When the pasta is done, drain well and place into a large bowl, add the cooked sausages, peppers, dressing, and spices.

5. Make sure you keep warm until ready to serve.

# Warm unexpected radish salad

Do not underestimate radishes, they can make quite a phenomenal salad. They may not be your favorite veggie to eat, but I am thinking after you experience this gourmet salad, you may just change your mind. At least, please give it a try and enjoy the uniqueness of the salad.

**Serving Size:** 2

**Cooking Time:** 20-25 Minutes

**Ingredients:**

- 1 cup sliced unpeeled radishes
- 1 Tbsp. olive oil
- ¼-cup walnuts
- Salt, white pepper
- 2 Tbsp. blue cheese dressing

**Instructions:**

1. Start by scrubbing and washing the radishes carefully.

2. Slice them very thin and then get the rest of the ingredients ready.

3. Heat the oil on medium in a medium pan, fry the radishes for 15 minutes, and season them.

4. When still warm, add the rest of the ingredients, combine and serve right away.

# Green and white, parsley and rice warm salad

This salad is going to be white, green and red. It may have the Christmas colors, but you do not have to wait for the holidays to prepare it or eat it. The green mainly creates by parsley, the white by rice, and the red by tomatoes.

**Serving Size:** 2

**Cooking Time:** 40 Minutes

**Ingredients:**

- 3 cups cooked white basmati rice
- 1 cups fresh minced parsley
- 1 cup diced fresh tomatoes
- 2 Tbsp. lemon juice
- 1 Tbsp. minced garlic
- 2 tbsp. diced white onion
- Salt, black pepper
- 1 tsp. ground cumin
- 2 Tbsp. olive oil

**Instructions:**

1. This is a great salad to make when you have leftover cooked rice.

2. In a large skillet, heat the oil and lemon juice on medium low temperature.

3. Add the parsley, garlic and onions. Cook them for about 5 minutes. Add the tomatoes. Stir well.

4. Finally, add the cooked rice and combine again.

5. You do not want to fry the rice, you just want to warm up all the ingredients together and serve this wonderful salad as a side warm salad.

# Salmond and citrus warm salad

This warm salad is just superb. Grill some fresh salmon, prepare a nice citrus vinaigrette, and add some orange slices, of course, on a bed of greens. It's also important to balance off the flavors by adding a little onions.

**Serving Size:** 3-4

**Cooking Time:** 50 Minutes

**For the dumplings:**

- 2 large fresh salmon filets
- 2 cups baby spinach leaves
- 2 cups fresh chopped arugula leaves
- 2 medium-size peeled oranges
- ½ cup shredded Parmesan cheese

**Dressing**

- 1 tbsp. Lemon juice
- 2 tbsp. olive oil
- ¼ cup orange juice
- ½ tsp. garlic powder
- Salt, black pepper

**Instructions:**

1. Preheat the oven to 375 degrees F. On a medium baking sheet, place the 2 salmon felts, skin down. Season with salt and paper, brush with oil and bake for 20 minutes.

2. In a small mixing bowl, combine the dressing ingredients and set aside.

3. Since the salmon is cooked, flake it with a fork.

4. Divide the mixed greens in 4 plates.

5. Also, divide the sliced oranges and the salmon into the 4 plates also.

6. Add the cheese on top of each salad and drizzle the dressing on top.

7. Enjoy fully!

# Warm pasta salad served in an avocado

This warm salad is impressive, but the presentation is really stands out the most at the end of the day. The cheese in the salad needs to melt easily and have enough of a strong taste to balance the avocado well. Let's start.

**Serving Size:** 4

**Cooking Time:** 20 Minutes

**Ingredients:**

- 2 large peeled avocados
- Some lemon juice
- 2 Tbsp. Greek salad dressing
- 3/4 cup shredded Mozzarella
- 1 cup diced cooked smoked ham
- 2 cups macaroni cooked noodles
- 2 Tbsp. chopped sundried tomatoes
- 2 Tbsp. sliced green olives

**Instructions:**

1. In a skillet, combine the salad dressing, oil, noodles and cheese.

2. Keep on low temperature just so the cheese melts. Add the sundried tomatoes and olives also.

3. Arrange the avocados. Cut them in half and pit them.

4. Sprinkle a little lemon juice on them so they do not get brownish.

5. Add the warm pasta salad in each avocados' half. Serve right away.

# Exceptional Greek warm salad

Greek salads are normally not served warm. If you order one in a restaurant, even a Greek restaurant, most likely, you will be served a bed of crispy cool bed of green with Feta cheese, olives, tomatoes, and more. We offer you a warm version of a Greek traditional salad, and we hope you will love this warm dish.

**Serving Size:** 4

**Cooking Time:** 30 Minutes

**Ingredients:**

- 2 chopped celery stalks
- ½ Tbsp. minced garlic
- 1 cup crumbled Feta cheese
- 1 cup chopped salami
- ½ cup diced seedless cucumbers
- Handful of sliced banana peppers
- 2 Tbsp. diced red onions
- 1/4cup Greek salad dressing, your favorite brand

**Instructions:**

1. In a large skillet, warm up the salad dressing on low.

2. Add the minced garlic, onions, cucumbers and celery and cook for 10 minutes.

3. Add the salami and the banana peppers and continue stirring, keeping it on low.

4. Serve with Feta cheese on top and enjoy as a light meal or a side salad.

# Beautiful bed of greens with fruits and warm crispy cheese.

Okay, we admit that we are slightly cheating here. The whole salad will not be warm. However, we can assure you that you will not be disappointed.

**Serving Size:** 4

**Cooking Time:** 45 Minutes

**Ingredients:**

- 4 thick slices of cheese Queso Blanco, you can buy as a block
- A little olive oil
- 2 large peeled grapefruit
- 4 cups mixed fresh greens
- ¼ cup roasted sunflowers
- 2 minced green onions

**Dressing:**

- 1 tbsp. Dijon mustard
- 1 Tbsp. minced garlic
- 1 tsp. red pepper flakes
- ¼ cup olive oil

**Instructions:**

1. Heat on medium-high temperature the olive n a large pan to be able to fry the cheese.

2. Meanwhile mix the dressing ingredients together and set aside.

3. Place the cheese in the pan and fry them for 5 minutes on each side.

4. Also, prepare the grapefruits, slicing them in small pieces and adding them to the mixed greens you will have previously divided in 4 plates.

5. Add also the roasted sunflowers. Place the completed fried large pieces of cheese on top of the bed of lettuce and add some homemade dressing.

6. Enjoy this beautiful salad as a perfect appetizer before a steak or grilled meat.

# Warm fried eggs salad.

Are you going to try this fried egg salad for breakfast? Yes, you can! You also can make your own menu anything you like. You can always make it a lunch option or even a delicious dinner, perhaps with a cup of soup. This is a great way to get a nice amount of proteins in a lighter meal.

**Serving Size:** 4

**Cooking Time:** 35 Minutes

**Ingredients:**

- 4 large eggs
- 2 cups baby spinach leaves
- 2 cups chopped kale
- 3 tbsp. diced red onions
- Few handful of garlic croutons
- Salt, pepper
- Olive oil
- Caesar salad dressing

**Instructions:**

1. Arrange and divide the mixed greens in 4 plates. Add the croutons and diced onions.

2. Next, it is time to fry your eggs.

3. Heat some olive oil; fry the eggs in a large pan easy over.

4. Season the eggs with salt and pepper.

5. Lay the fried eggs on top of each bed of salad.

6. Add a generous portion of Caesar salad dressing and dig in!

# Goat cheese will warm up your heart

I do not know if you ever tried warm, baked goat cheese. This recipe will propose a great way to try it. Good cheese has a unique taste and is loved by everyone.

**Serving Size:** 4

**Cooking Time:** 35 Minutes

**Ingredients:**

- large log of goat cheese, sliced thick in 4
- 4 cups mixed green, iceberg and arugula perhaps or any mixed greens you like
- ¼ cup chopped walnuts
- 1 Tbsp. unsalted butter
- 1 tbsp. honey
- 2 tbsp. orange zest

**Dressing**

- 2 Tbsp. balsamic vinegar
- 6 tbsp. olive oil
- 2 tbsp. orange juice
- 1 Tbsp. minced garlic

**Instructions:**

1. In a small bowl, combine the ingredients for the dressing and set aside.

2. Heat the butter with the honey in a medium pan and add the 4 thick slices of goat cheese, about 5 minutes-6 minutes on each side.

3. Divide the mixed greens in 4 portions. Add the orange zest and walnuts on each plate and add the fried goat cheese on top,

4. Finalize with the dressing on top.

# Conclusion

We are already done! Time flies when we are having a great time! To us, preparing some warm salads is almost like creating a piece of art. Let us combine the perfect ingredients together, most of the time well balanced. It is important to try to have some produce representation, proteins, dairy products, and grains or nuts. Of course, this is if you are not vegetarian. If you are avoiding meat, you can still make your salad filled with proteins by adding some beans, tofu or cheese, and nuts.

I used to think as a child that salads were awful and you would often only eat them loaded with croutons and swimming in Caesar or ranch dressing. That should not be the only way to introduce salads or warms salads to your kids. Make sure you do show otherwise to your little ones.

With my children, I early on involved them in the kitchen. I make salads fun! How can you do so? Let them pick some of the ingredients! Line up on the counter some suggested ingredients you want to choose from. Propose some Feta cheese, black olives, and grapes tomatoes for a Greek-style salad. If you have everything to make a buffalo chicken salad, let them pick the best spicy sauce to their taste, blue cheese crumbs or just simple shredded Mozzarella and fried dried onions or kernel corn. If you know your little ones love tuna, let them mix it with mayonnaise, little celery salt, and some dill pickles or garlic pickles, depending on their favorites. Again, it is all about involving them. One of my nieces will eat any type of salads if it contains fruits. It is very easy to mix fruits and savory ingredients, such as berries and grilled flank steak or mandarins, and fried chicken. You just keep introducing them options they may like and soon enough, they will ask for salads often when you least expect it.

Warm salads are delicious, colorful, pretty, and nutritious. We all wish someone would serve us homemade warm salad every night, without having to make it. Until you actually realize they are not as complicated to make as everyone is making it seem.

# About the Author

Ivy's mission is to share her recipes with the world. Even though she is not a professional cook she has always had that flair toward cooking. Her hands create magic. She can make even the simplest recipe tastes superb. Everyone who has tried her food has astounding their compliments was what made her think about writing recipes.

She wanted everyone to have a taste of her creations aside from close family and friends. So, deciding to write recipes was her winning decision. She isn't interested in popularity, but how many people have her recipes reached and touched people. Each recipe in her cookbooks is special and has a special meaning in her life. This means that each recipe is created with attention and love. Every ingredient carefully picked, every combination tried and tested.

Her mission started on her birthday about 9 years ago, when her guests couldn't stop prizing the food on the table. The next thing she did was organizing an event where chefs from restaurants were tasting her recipes. This event gave her the courage to start spreading her recipes.

She has written many cookbooks and she is still working on more. There is no end in the art of cooking; all you need is inspiration, love, and dedication.

# Author's Afterthoughts

I am thankful for downloading this book and taking the time to read it. I know that you have learned a lot and you had a great time reading it. Writing books is the best way to share the skills I have with your and the best tips too.

I know that there are many books and choosing my book is amazing. I am thankful that you stopped and took time to decide. You made a great decision and I am sure that you enjoyed it.

I will be even happier if you provide honest feedback about my book. Feedbacks helped by growing and they still do. They help me to choose better content and new ideas. So, maybe your feedback can trigger an idea for my next book.

Thank you again


Sincerely

Ivy Hope

Printed in Great Britain
by Amazon